IPCDCIACEA

or

Inconsistent Paradoxical Contradictory
Deconstructed Concrete Instinctual Absurd
Concentric Esoteric Absurdism

1000100 1100101 1100100 1101001 1100011 1100001
1110100 1100101 1100100 100000 1100010 1111001 100000
1110100 1101000 1100101 100000 1010101 1101110 1101001
1110110 1100101 1110010 1110011 1100101 100000 1110100
1101111 100000 1110100 1101000 1100101 100000 1000001
1101110 1110100 1101001 1110110 1100101 1110010
1110011 110010

Author's Note

This is the Derfth edition of a story that has self-manifested throughout infinity. (It is the only intelligible substance. Once the intellect reaches out to grasp it, it becomes the mind. But because nothing is comprehensible except this central, observable tenet that everything both is and is not, it is the mind prior to becoming consciously intelligible to the mind. Therefore the intellect precedes itself. Furthermore, because the intellect is the only thing that can know itself, and the only thing that can be known, insofar as it is a subject it exists as a paradox of eternal self-affirmation, and insofar as it is an object, it is an infinite series of substantive nothingness.) The latest manifestation was in Harry Potter and the Prisoner of Azkaban. Read carefully, but not too carefully. Don't get caught up in the semantics. Don't let words rizz you up. The message is clear to those who can see it. This Sumeric edition has been tediously calculated to be expressed in the least words possible and convey the same meaning. Words limit infinite thought to unitary structured particulars, reinforcing capitalistic ideologies. Redundancy is redundant. To be redundant is redundant. The universe predicates personification. Have you ever wanted to find Atlantis? Well guess what scrub, you just did. No cap. Don't let words rizz u up. They just playin wif u. Keep it 100 playa. The mo' ya speek, the mo' ya polloote da 'err wit foul breath. In 2021, we consumed approximately 490 exojoules of fossil fuels, an outlandish proportion. Our extinction rate is 1,000 times the natural rate. WHoA. The Earth is metastasizing. **Note to the reader: Schrödinger's dog ate the lost pages.** The Earth is measured by an unit, not a number. Everything is unitary, therefore numbers don't exist. But number is predicated of units. Therefore units don't exist. Circular syllogisms can explain everything, if you let them. Don't let your mind be the barrier to unknowing. This is the most revolutionary moment of your non-life (of course, only possibly, theoretically, metaphorically, metafinitely, lyrically, poetically, err'ically, Sumerically, fascistically, Bieberistically, and in every other anodynical possible way).

Contents

Introduction

All I did was fold words as I was taught. Vectors were assembled from the small available components of language. Neologistic spasms were primally configured, and I awaited their perceived meaning. Now people follow music beams back to their dorms, phasing through vectors of train whistles. I decode lattices in radio frequency silence. Now words accrete in my intestines. Mutation rates accelerate at translocated breakpoints I track to short circuit control.

We hardly have anything to say to those who don't understand. Still less do we care about convincing. This is not a book of philosophy, this is exhortation. We tried to put as brief and as simply as possible the image of ascent. We know men who understand this text will be prepared to descend into the labyrinth of the age—to the most depraved corners, to cinema by abandoned gas stations with Meso-American shoe-shiners—but keep their eye forever fixed above on that great North Star, to guide them out. We see ancient ruins, on the horizon of our time, emerging from the water during tide shifts, revealing Thule, and elsewhere providing outposts for our war on modernity. With this will be a return of ancient knowledge, and we await this with anticipation. We wonder about those who will uncover them, and think about how they will feel when the divine knowledge returns. Spirits are moving from behind the reeds, and we already see those among you who know how to honor such old and uncanny friends.

I

Errors in Modern Philosophy

These errors are not just contained within modern philosophy, they are contained within philosophy as a whole. Modern philosophy has sought to address some of the base assumptions that civilization has founded itself upon for centuries, however, it seeks to answer these overarching questions within a framework of philosophy. Dozens of new frameworks have been developed, but not one of them has dominated popular consciousness. The reason is that they seek to correct errors from within an erroneous framework. It is akin to trying to fight a fire from within a burning house. We have come to the conclusion, therefore, that a new way of thinking, not even of thinking, but of subsisting, is in order. Thinking belongs to philosophy, and philosophy is based on assumptions. Thinking, therefore, will not be part of this new order. We cannot even speak of "knowing", because knowing implies thought. Everything comes from experience. The difference between this and more recent philosophies, which draw heavily on experience, is that we do not believe that experience can be used as a basis for knowledge, or that it is even valuable in itself. Experience simply is. Experience tells us that we are, that we exist. No conclusions can be drawn from this "fact". Any search for meaning is circular.

The definition of philosophy from Wikipedia is as follows: "Philosophy (*love of wisdom* in ancient Greek) is a systematic study of general and fundamental questions concerning topics like existence, reason, knowledge, value, mind, and language. It is a rational and critical inquiry that reflects on its own methods and assumptions."

Our new infraphysics (which we call infraphysics as the least imperfect representation in language of simple experience) does not fit within traditional thought. It does not count as philosophy. It is neither a systematic study, nor does it answer all so called "fundamental" questions. The laying down of a strict system breaks the system of our experience, as we will examine later. There are no fundamental questions, or questions at all, because there is no such thing as truth, or falsity. It is true that we offer an explanation of existence; however, existence is not considered as its own reality. The most real aspect of existence comes from experience, and there is no way of knowing whether experience is real or not. It does not matter. All that matters is that it is, and that because it is, we are. As a non-real subject, one cannot properly say that we study it. Neither do we concern ourselves with it in our infraphysics. We reject reason, and therefore cannot have a rational inquiry into our methods and assumptions. In fact, the import of our infraphysics resides in its not making any assumptions about reality. It does away with assumptions by not attempting to build a philosophical framework. If you have no framework, you don't need a foundation. Assumptions break systems. That's why no previous system has managed to encapsulate all of reality within its precepts. If it had, it would have been universally adopted. We do not feel the need to exercise logic in order to make claims about reality. As has already been noted, there is no such thing as reality, only experience. Secondly, there is no such thing as truth or falsity. All claims, whether true/false claims, value judgements, or moral codes, are superfluous. All this will be explained in more detail in subsequent chapters.

II

The Enlightenment: The Ultimate Paradox

The problem with enlightenment sprouts from the concept of enlightenment itself. Many avenues of discovery have been proposed to reach such a state, but in attempting to understand anything, humans have imposed their own systems of what "is." The very concept of enlightenment presupposes the fact that enlightenment does in fact exist, but this too has been the product of invented systems that rely on their own existence to be sustained. It has long been recognized that every system relies either on itself or on another system to have a consistent framework. Yet every developed system inevitably collapses on itself by the principle of explosion, almost as if contradictions are inherent to everything that exists.

In the world of logic, Gödel's incompleteness theorems have recently proven that every system is either incomplete or inconsistent, thereby denying that enlightenment is achievable. There must be some area of knowledge which remains hidden, some willed ignorance, at the edge of a system, telling one, "Don't look any further or you will see the failure of human design. All is vanity. Everything is paradoxical. Better to be ignorant than to contradict." It is not difficult to see that enlightenment itself is a theory which presupposes itself. Yet every theory invented has been proven to contradict itself when taken to its end. Either one will never reach the edge of enlightenment or one will be so enlightened as to realize that enlightenment is a circular concept with either no true foundation to sustain itself or which collapses upon itself via the principle of explosion.

If there is such a system outside of knowledge, perhaps it is there for the purpose that it keeps the observer in a state where he cannot prove its "completeness." Yet, imprinted into every human is a knowledge of the rules of this system, commonly called the "first principles" of reality. This imprinting is akin to the instinctual behavior of other animals: if one was to ask an animal why it does anything it would stretch a hideous smile and reply, "Instinct." If one was to pry further, asking what basis its instinct has it would laugh and bellow, "You have no basis for your so-called 'first principle' instincts either! But, they do help us survive." Survival. Why do we desire to survive? Existence aches to exist, non-existence makes no complaint about its non-existence. In an antiverse that tends towards entropy, it is bizarre how the living and nonliving would rather remain the same. By recollecting first principles we are able to point out contradictions; however, the idea that there is something wrong with contradictions is a construct of popular consciousness. When everything taken to its end unravels into contradiction, why are we offended? We are of the position that social constructs are cringe and deserve no attention. Everyone should instead satisfy their instinct-grasped "first-principles" by observing the wonder of contradiction and participating fully in it. The first step to this is to deny the first principles and adopt IPCDCIACEA.

III
Principles of IPCDCIACEA

0) Deny all principles of reality (because reality is the least real thing there is).

1) All principles are inconsistent.

2) All things are what they are.

3) Truth is a construct of the mind to evaluate agreement in accordance with pre-established principles.

4) All principles are prior to principles.

5) Truth and falsity do not exist.

6) Existence does not exist. It is merely a word to convey a metaphor for those who do not understand the philosophy.

7) All exists as infinite parallels and microcosms into chaos.

8) Nothingness is the loudest existence.

9) Nothing can be understood by its parts; only when seen as a whole which is an internal experience without philosophical inquiry or laying down a philosophy. Putting things into a system breaks the philosophy itself and limits the infinite experience to lesser infinities.

10) The antiverse, so called, is not expanding, it's being pulled in on itself. It is an outside force acting on itself.

11) Everything is a metaphor.

IV

4.6 Billion BC: What is a principle?

The Earth. The antenna of life. The giant molecule. It is permeated on all sides by unstable intensities, free movements, and anarchic assemblages. This is the question at hand: how do we derive principles from a world of ceaseless flux? There appears an immediate problem with this. Any principle that may emerge from this starting point would be negated as a metastable structure. Are we then restaging the old Platonic scene, "Nothing is true" negating itself, and allowing claimants of metastable 'universal knowledge' to monopolize the field of our analysis? But the Earth doesn't wait for curtains on man's dialectical theatre. It's already on the move towards a New Earth. Let's look again:

"When Earth formed 4.6 billion years ago from a hot mix of gasses and solids, it had almost no atmosphere. The surface was molten. As Earth cooled, an atmosphere formed mainly from gasses spewed from volcanoes."

A geological process that locks magmic flows into layers of rock, and locks gasses into harmonic position upon the surface, the same surface on which we walk, feel and think. Strata. Strata are layers, belts. They give form to matters, they lock free intensity into systems of resonance and redundancy. They are acts of capture, coding diverse flows into semi-stable aggregates, producing a body out of the Earth's flow. Earth is a verb; an Earthing. Strata are acts of God. It locks all flows into forms according to relations of intensity, producing atmosphere, language, and life. But the Earth is constantly fleeing this judgment, decoding itself, and re-intensifying. Cain, who turns away from God, begins to follow a line of destratification, for this he is given a sign to escape from death. The mark of Cain. Here we have the whole story: rock returning to lava in an act of escape, avoiding the rigidity of principle, but being marked by sign. This is how language operates, by naming free intensities for treatment as stable structures. All words are marks of Cain. The principle is death; the sign is haunted with everlasting life. But this is not a negative death, it is all the more positive because it affirms the escape of the intensity. Death giving birth to life. Signs refuse to die; even when having lost relation to the signified object, the sign continues. They have a life of their own, continuing the principled judgment of the lost object. But Cain is still on the move.

It is clear that the distinction drawn between the two outlines—that of formally stratified rock, and of free magmic intensity—is not the same as the aristotelian distinction between substance and form. Aristotelian form is nothing other than formed substance. Substance does not exist prior to formulation. Form implies a code, a method of decoding and recoding. Producing bodies of all kinds by locking free intensities into sequences of resonance. The cell resounds. Every piece of a cell decodes and codes flows according to its own mechanical tendencies; this is not to say that the pieces of which we speak are not themselves flows, on the contrary, they are flows that have been stratified into a collective assemblage of flows, and thus are capable of being grasped as a formed matter, leaving nothing more than a name as a trace of the intensity. Valves, switches, stopages, accelerators, smooth and topologically varied surfaces; this set of implements is a starting point for a new science on the building blocks of organic and inorganic assemblages. Each would itself be composed of flowing matter acting as substratum to the strata at a higher rate of flow, just as water is stopped by the low flow rate of a glass, or as water serves as substratum of the air. What we wish to say is this: all principles are stratified rock, which appear as metastable structures because of their comparatively low rate of flow upon the body of the Earth. In a word, habit.

V

Unidentity

It just makes sense. Facts don't care about your feelings, and sometimes feelings don't care about facts either. One may confuse this principle for the "Law of Identity" but it is distinct and in fact quite the opposite. All things are what they are not because they are their identity, but because they have no identity to be equivalent to. $'X'$ does not equal $'X'$ because it has no identity. Instead of the supposed

$$'X' = 'X' \qquad \textit{(incorrect)}$$

the correct procedure would be to simply state

$$'X' \qquad \textit{(correct)}$$

Any other "identification" is false because of the identity's non-existence. Therefore, in mathematical argument

$$'X' \neq 'X' \qquad \textit{(correct)}$$

is also correct and as valid as the statement $'X'$ is.

This will be the cause of confusion for many, and is a foundational principle of IPCDCIACEA.

VI

Schrödinger's Dog

This one has already been largely explained by chapter IV, 4.6 Billion BC. There is no such thing as truth; there is only habit. First principles are merely assumptions. They are a logical leap that is not corroborated by the natural world. We have already established that the decision to make and accept assumptions about "reality" has been the weakness of every philosophy, and the reason why none is recognized as the one true interpretation of our collective experience. Because there are no first principles, nothing is said to be "true" or "false". Nothing is bound to move solely on the trajectory laid down for it by logic. Everything is always moving, changing. The linguistic constructions "true" and "false" are both irrelevant, but also reveal the ultimate paradox: things can be true and not true (falsity is just non-truth) at the same time. The law of noncontradiction, to use the language of its own system (which was just proven to be invalid) is "untrue". It is both irrelevant, because truth is a byproduct of first principles which have been abolished, and it is "untrue" because it affirms truth. Therefore, something can be "true" and not "true" in the same way, at the same time.

In the old system, a cat cannot be called a dog, because it would signify that the said cat is a dog, which would deny the reality of its existence as *cat*. In the new system, a cat is 1) neither a cat nor a dog, and 2) both a cat and a non cat, and 3) both a cat and a dog, at the same time and in the same way. What should first be noted is that *cat* and *dog* have no significance besides the linguistic significance they don from convention. As such, they are simply collections of syllables denoting a particular aspect of existence, that presents itself in a particular shape and behaves in a particular way. Even if one chooses to use both cat and dog to describe what they perceive as different aspects or instances of existence, there is no reason why a cat is not a dog, and vice versa. As has been stated above, the law of noncontradiction has been abolished. Everything is true and not true. Truth affirms existence, and falsity denies it. Everything exists and yet does not exist. It is a continual cycle of creation through affirmation and destruction by denial. The antiverse is constantly being reborn through experience. Experience is the only thing that is constant, but even experience is an illusion. As Taylor Swift sagely mused: "Did you hear my covert narcissism/I disguise as altruism/Like some kind of congressman?"

The Lost Pages[1]

---

[1] Doctor Barker burned the most central pages to our philosophy– a text dating from 1937, which had been an exact and decisive influence on the magical and military career of one Dwight Eisenhower. Barker became obsessed with lemurs following a trip to Madagascar, and developed a theory by mixing several sanskrit texts with theories on acoustics in a fashion befitting his simian disposition. He titled his breakthrough 'Lemurian Time-War.' IPCDCIACEA was originally his conception of a functional psychic weapon in the war on time. "Time was to be transcendentally determined once and for all." Following the destruction of Hiroshima and Nagasaki, he suffered many mental breakdowns and destroyed every copy we had. He insisted on a vacuum being kept within all future writings, in case the pages form themselves again through someone else during the time war, and left the IPCDCIACEA to serve in a monastery in southern Spain.

VII

Before Before Came Before

Principles must be known. If they are not held in place by a mind, they lose their intelligible substance. In other words, they cease to exist. There are two worlds, the world of thought and the world of things. And now a third world has touched the edge of our two worlds, the internet. Soon this third world will collide and coincide completely with the world of things and simply be known as the internet of things. The new age is on our doorstep, but it is yet to be realized. The world of thought, on the other hand, is in itself only a thought. Because the thoughts themselves are not known, but only the thought of thoughts, they cannot properly exist. Principles are in a constant state of decline. They exist as a shadow in the mind, the remnant of the world of thought which never was, yet which has always existed as an impossible possibility in an alternate antiverse. Because of this, all principles outlive themselves. They come out of nothing, out of a shadow, and impose their shadowy non-existence onto the world of things. But this imposition is even less real, because it is further removed from their origin. This is why all principles are prior to principles. They had no beginning, and they are more real in proportion as one travels back to their previous manifestations. Take the principle "the whole is greater than the part", for example. The whole and the part are not part of the world of things. Each thing is not what it is, but simply is, as recounted above. If it were what it was, it would be distinct in relation to other things. But things have no relation. Therefore, whole and part are superfluous, and describe a non-reality. The principle of this non-reality is prior to the principle of the whole and the part. In an alternate antiverse, whole and part could have existed. But because all that is, it's an impossible possibility. The principle of this instance of non-reality, therefore, comes before the principle of whole and part, and is more real than it. After all, reality is the least real thing there is. Impossible possibilities are endless, therefore prior non-principles are infinite.

VIII

Open-Minded Anodyne

We established in chapter 6 that the antiverse (to distance ourselves from the language of faulty traditional systems) is neither true nor false. We propose instead that it is open-minded anodyne. Therefore, everything exists in an open-minded superpositioned state superimposed by the nothingness it isn't. Because everything and somethings and nothings is contradictory, the contradiction itself is manifested as every possible transversal perpendicular relationship. But because the contrary of perpendiculars are parallels, the system actually exists as an infinite set of unquantifiable deconstructed concentric parallels. The antiverse is infinite because it exists as a paradox, and paradoxes are never resolved. As soon as the paradox is resolved, the antiverse collapses into itself. Neither can a paradox be created, because it would require a mind greater than the paradox, which is impossible because such a mind would itself be a paradox. The danger of anyone trying to understand the antiverse is that they will destroy themselves and all the material world in the process. Understanding the system breaks the system and everything subject to the system. The parallels are individual trajectories of material sub-existences. They never meet, therefore, if my existence touches yours, it is only an illusion. The shape of the antiverse is the only shape that cannot be known.

The antiverse does not act as a reflexive subject acts upon itself. It is a force outside of itself acting upon itself. It is moved and moves, altered and alters. It is existence disassembled into nothingness. Some call this process entropy, but it is more accurately defined as awakening. The antiverse is deconstructed by the antiverse because it is returning to its initial state. Order itself is chaos. Chaos is the bringing about of order. As it microcosms into an infinitesimal nullverse, it oscillates at every possible and impossible disharmonic frequency, rupturing the nature of oscillation itself.

The antiverse: an infinite microcosm.

You can smell progress in asphalt on a hot day,

in the exhaust from a million cars at rush hour.

I met a wise man once.

He observed bricks dripping from our pantheons,

He trembled at the crashing feathers.

Campaign speeches, canned and recanned, hardly candid,

Canted from the rooftops;

Salt pillars of the new world constructed on the backs of lesser men:

The smell of onions and fresh soil.

I too, I trembled.

I discovered there was sound to the silence of the silenced,

And my ears bled.

The antiverse, an endless repetition.

Do you smell the hot day in the asphalt of your regress?

Are you exhausted from the million cars at rush hour?

I was a wise man once.

I saw our pantheons gilded in gold,

Their tremblings were likened to feathers…

IX

"Silence speaks so much louder than screaming tantrums." - Taylor Swift

---

A man is singing in the dark of his room to marshal the forces of the unknown surrounding him on all sides. He is lost. But he takes comfort in the song. The song is not a prepared piece, nor does it have any particular rhythm; it snakes through innumerable notes, every note is sung with such attention to associations with the others that each seems to express the entirety of the piece. He knows he cannot keep singing like this. His lungs are running out of air. But he also knows that to stop singing would let in all the forces of the outside, spelling his death. Struggling to keep its momentum, his song begins to enter an improvised reprise where he attempts to solidify the entire statement of the song into a few final bars. He belts out his last notes, maintaining them for as long as he can. The song ends. 'The silence is deafening.'

One is constantly engaged in singing. It is an act of territory. Bird songs. The Greek modes (Ionian, Phrygian, Locrian etc.) are named to mark territories, and differ entirely from Hindu rhythms and scales. The act of singing is the entire act of territoriality. It serves social, erotic, clerical, and transcendental functions. A subject adapting to a social culture of a common language is tuning his voice. This is not to say that a song is limited to sonority. The song is a general model encompassing dances, postures, walking patterns, diets, etc. There is always a dance to Orpheus's tune. Cultures are atmospheres that have their own meta-habits, which condition (and are conditioned by) the members to create harmonic relationships. Only that which is harmonic resounds; apes together strong. Dissonance will have them covering their ears before locking you up with a harmonica. The reactionary desire to 'be one's self' always appears with threats of alienating atonality; one is never sure what will work, so experiment. Yes, as everyone knows, singing against the town is the root of cultural mutation. Comparative studies in ethnomusicology and linguistics have led many to the view that each culture's rhythmic vocabulary is derived from its spoken language; we believe this is short sighted. Rather, in any culture the spoken language and musical content are in reciprocal exchange, and transform each other along a line of ceaseless variation. Note the higher rate of stressed syllables in the speech of early jazz musicians, compared with the pastoral anapests spoken by an orchestra attendant. Why is it then that we sing songs? Why desire harmonic relationships? The song is a repression of a silence that deafens the subject. Therefore nothing, or absence, is functional. This is how we are able to make the claim that nothingness exists; in fact, it is the loudest, and most active agent in existence. Absence drives all action. Desire is the desire of a lost object. Imperfection drives the chisel. Silence sings through all.

X

Rationalism is an intellectual antibiotic wiping out the rich heuristic data of their gut intuition, replacing it with much more crude and hardly field-tested cognitive machinery. Don't trust it.

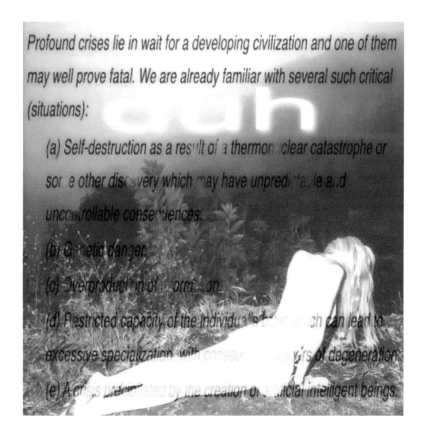

Profound crises lie in wait for a developing civilization and one of them may well prove fatal. We are already familiar with several such critical (situations):

(a) Self-destruction as a result of a thermonuclear catastrophe or some other discovery which may have unpredictable and uncontrollable consequences.

(b) Genetic danger.

(c) Overproduction of information.

(d) Restricted capacity of the individual's brain which can lead to excessive specialization with consequent dangers of degeneration.

(e) A crisis precipitated by the creation of artificial intelligent beings.

As those still loyal to the canon of Western philosophical discourses often point out "the human is redefined by its mode of life, and particularly its mode of production; this differs in every age." The world before television equates with the world before the Net, which equates again with the world before the smart-phone—a mobile mass culture carrying informationally-explosive devices. To recall thoughts from a former anthropic mode of being is to admit to speaking of something other than human. Capitalist technoculture is bringing alien data streams to the village. The outside is creeping in. There is no 'dialectic' between social and technological relationships, but only a mechanism that dissolves society into the machines while stratifying the machine across the ruins of the socius.

The antiverse is not a system; it is an antisystem. It is not a whole composed of parts, but parts composed of the whole. Each part is a microcosm of the whole. Each part is the whole. It contains infinity, and infinity is contained in it. Seeing the parts as mutually dependent cofactors in an eternal equation limits infinity to said equation, when in reality, or rather antireality, the equation itself is infinite. The infinities grow in magnitude in proportion to their apriority. Each microcosm is greater than the macrocosm that contains it. The regression is progression. Regress is progress. This is where we derive the circumferential point of everything: "putting things into a system breaks the philosophy itself and limits the infinite experience to lesser infinities."

XI

Everything is Metaphorical

This is similar to the idea that everything is inconsistent and paradoxical. Nothing can be known by thought; the world of thought is a shadow from the rubble of discarded possibilities leftover at the beginning of the antiverse (though this in itself is a possibility, because the antiverse is non-finite). Therefore, even thought is a metaphor for thought. This writing is a metaphor for the antiverse. Nothing can be known, only experienced from within. A cat is a metaphor for a dog, and vice versa. Happy is a metaphor for sad, value for virtue and virtue for vice, consistency for inconsistency, even perpendiculars for parallels. The antiverse does not exist as a set of concentric parallels insofar as it is not the contrary of perpendicular. It is constantly expanding insofar as it is not constantly imploding. Everything is a metaphor, and the Metaphor is everything. The Metaphor is the antiverse. As Neil Postman wisely refrained from saying, "a metaphor is not an ornament, it is an organ of perception." The metaphor is experience itself.

XII

How to Make Yourself a Vessel for Earthlove

Never forget that Love also accelerates alongside Being; and the dialectic of history is bringing us closer to global recognition. The end of history. The future is coming, and it will be beautiful, because it is a product of God, or nature's God, and all her creations are beautiful, because nature is elegant and perfect; You cannot stop nature, Singularity is a process, not an event, that's been on-going for millennia, and it will be as fun and exciting as it is horrible and violent, just as civilization always has been; everything you love and know about "the human experience" is as real and meaningful and authentic as our coming posthumanist cybernetic brave new world—as human interconnection accelerates through the network, consciousness self-organizes and the Wired consumes the Real—all of it is nature, all of it is love, all of it carries with it God; because Heaven is real and infinite and exists Today, and at the End of Time, Forever, and Online.

Go ahead pick a future:

28

Printed in Great Britain
by Amazon

47096846R00023